THE NEW METHOD FOR AFRO-CUBAN DRUMMING

Executive Producers
Rob Wallis and Paul Siegel

◆

Book Design and Production
Dancing Planet® MediaWorks™

◆

Photography
Rob Shanahan

◆

Audio CD Examples Recorded and Performed by
Jimmy Branly
Alberto Salas plays piano on tracks 93 and 94.
Jorge Perez "Sawa" plays bass on tracks 93 and 94.
Jimmy also plays bass on tracks 96 and 97.

◆

Transcriptions of Jimmy's Musical Examples
Neftaly Gonzalez

Catalog# HL6620087 and HD-BK06

HUDSON MUSIC®

About the Author

Jimmy Branly, born in Havana, Cuba, has played with Afro-Cuban greats such as Cuarto Espacio, Hernan Lopez, Gonzalo Rubalcaba, Issac Delgado, and NG La Banda. In the United States he has performed with the Sheila E. band, the L.A. Latin Jazz All-Star Big Band, Bill Wolfer (Mambo-rama), Russell Ferrante, Jimmy Haslip, the Sandro Albert Quintet, Airto Moreira and Flora Purim, the Carlos Cuevas Trio, the Brandon Fields Group, Otmaro Ruiz, Luis Conte, Mike Turre, Raul Malo, Celia Cruz, Bayalo, Tito Nieves, Albita Rodriguez, Strunz and Farah, Susie Hansen, Rebecca Mauleon, and his own Jimmy Branly Band. Jimmy endorses Yamaha drums and hardware, Zildjian cymbals and sticks, Remo heads, and LP percussion.

Acknowledgments

I want to thank all of the great musicians who helped and influenced me in the music scene back in Cuba: Daniel Peraza (the one who made me switch from sports to music), Enrique Pla (from Irakere, and one of my great drum teachers), Omar Hernandez, Hernan Lopez Nussa, Fernando Calveiro, Jose Luis "El Tosco" (NG La Banda), Issac Delgado, Charly Flores, and the late, great "Yulo." My first classical percussion teacher, Arnoldo. The teacher of all of us living outside Cuba, Roberto Concepcion (ha, ha, ha). Ernesto Simpson, Geraldo Piloto (a great drummer and composer from the group Klimax), Gonzalo Rubalcaba (for teaching me how to play soft), Felipe Cabrera. All my love goes to my mother and my big and beautiful family for their love and support in my career.

Here in the United States everything changes for Cubans. There are many other types of music and concepts that make us understand the world in a different way. Back in Cuba we had all day to play music and practice. Now we have other responsibilities besides music, and it is beautiful to see a future you can build on your own.

There are many great musicians back in Cuba, real talent that no one knows, my best wishes for them. Thanks to all the great drummers in the United States, musicians that influenced me back then and now, such as: Neil Peart (the first drummer I ever heard), Ringo Starr, Elvin Jones, Dennis Chambers, Buddy Rich, Tony Williams, Vinnie Colaiuta, Ian Pace, Jeff "Tain" Watts, Horacio "El Negro" Hernandez, Bill Stewart, Gregg Bissonette, Ignacio Berroa, and many others. Thanks to Chuck Silverman and Terry O'Mahoney for their support back in Cuba and here in the United States. Thanks to Joe Testa at Yamaha for their great drums and hardware, Kirsten Matt at Zildjian for their cymbals and sticks, Matt Connors at Remo heads, and Martin Cohen at LP.

I especially want to thank my beautiful wife Alondra for her love and support.

My special thanks to Neftaly Gonzales, who worked with me on this book night and day. With all my heart, thanks to Rob Wallis, Paul Siegel, and Hudson Music .

Table Of Contents

Introduction

Welcome to *The New Method for Afro-Cuban Drumming*. In this book I've put together examples of my style of playing drum set. You'll find that there are not many names or styles mentioned (i.e., songo, timba, mambo). This book and my playing represent a fusion of all these styles. Every example you will read and listen to (all exercises are recorded) is taken from my little box of experiences which I brought from Cuba.

Here in the United States I have been exposed to many musical concepts. I find myself playing a bit differently from when I first arrived, inspired by being in the United States, and learning so much from the musicians with whom I've performed. This is what I will share with you as well.

My concept came primarily from listening to jazz. Jazz has helped me to think more musically. *The New Method for Afro-Cuban Drumming* is for all drummers who do not necessarily want to learn the authentic way of Cuban-style drumming but more a fusion of these styles. Please remember that this is only my way of playing. There are many other drummers, Cubans and non-Cubans, who play these styles amazingly. Each one has a particular voice and concept. I hope that my style and concepts help to answer some of your questions.

Clave is a word and concept that most drummers, I find, take too seriously. That being said, you as the drummer are responsible for this element. It can be musically and rhythmically danger-ous if you don't interpret the clave in the right way. What is the right way? You can answer this question yourself if you listen to music and dedicate some time to analyzing the styles of Cuban music. Then you'll be more likely to understand the clave and its role. But, don't take it too personally or too seriously. Sometimes it's the people you're playing with who will direct where the clave is going to be. Many times you will share the stage with musicians who don't know the style as well as you do. Then it is your responsibility to make them sound good. If you don't feel the clave in the right place, don't force it. The Cuban clave is very strong and it can be as beautiful as it can be ugly if not interpreted and played the right way. The cáscara pattern can sometimes do the job of the clave rhythm by itself (without the need to state the clave), and this can be further helped by adding some of the bass drum examples presented in Chapter 3. All of these examples will work perfectly with almost any bass or piano tumbáo.

In this book you will hear the clave change from son to rumba. This has been done to emphasize the musical fact that the rhythmic patterns work well with both claves.

Example 58 in the book is a combination of bass drum patterns that fit with the clave. You can use this example in many different ways. Practice all of the examples in a variety of ways. Play them "as is," play them as two-bar phrases, read them from the end to the beginning, and make up your own combinations and phrases. Make sure you play musically when you are performing these patterns.

The concept of *The New Method for Afro-Cuban Drumming* is to help you modernize Afro-Cuban styles and fuse them into your own style. Within this book you may find patterns you recognize and others that you do not. Don't worry about names. Just learn the examples and add them to your own concept of playing drums.

Words of Advice

The best advice I can give to all drummers and percussionists who really want to learn these styles is to listen to the music carefully. Don't just listen to the drums. Listen to every single detail of every instrument. This is the best way to understand the concept of communication between instruments. Second, listen to as much music as you can, from Latin-jazz and straight ahead jazz, to salsa, son, and timba. These styles have been played for years by great musicians from all around the world.

I hope this book will help you in some way. There are many more ideas that can be added to these examples. Just be creative, musical, and always respect the language and authenticity of all musical styles.

Respectfully,
Jimmy Branly

Technique Tips

These pictures show a technique used by many timbaleros that can also be applied to the drum set. Pressing the index finger onto the stick as you strike the head muffles the drum sound. The same technique can be applied to the shell of the floor tom or the cowbell.

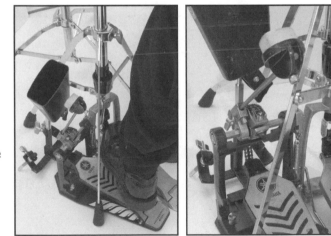

Here is how I play the cowbell with the pedal when I want both the sound of the bell and the hi-hat. Notice that I slide the heel of the foot to the left in order to play the cowbell.

This picture shows what you can do to any pedal that you are using to play the cowbell next to the hi-hat. Take the beater on the right side of the sprocket and move it to the left side of the sprocket, this will allow the beater motion to move freely, without being hindered by the leg of the hi-hat stand.

Notation Key

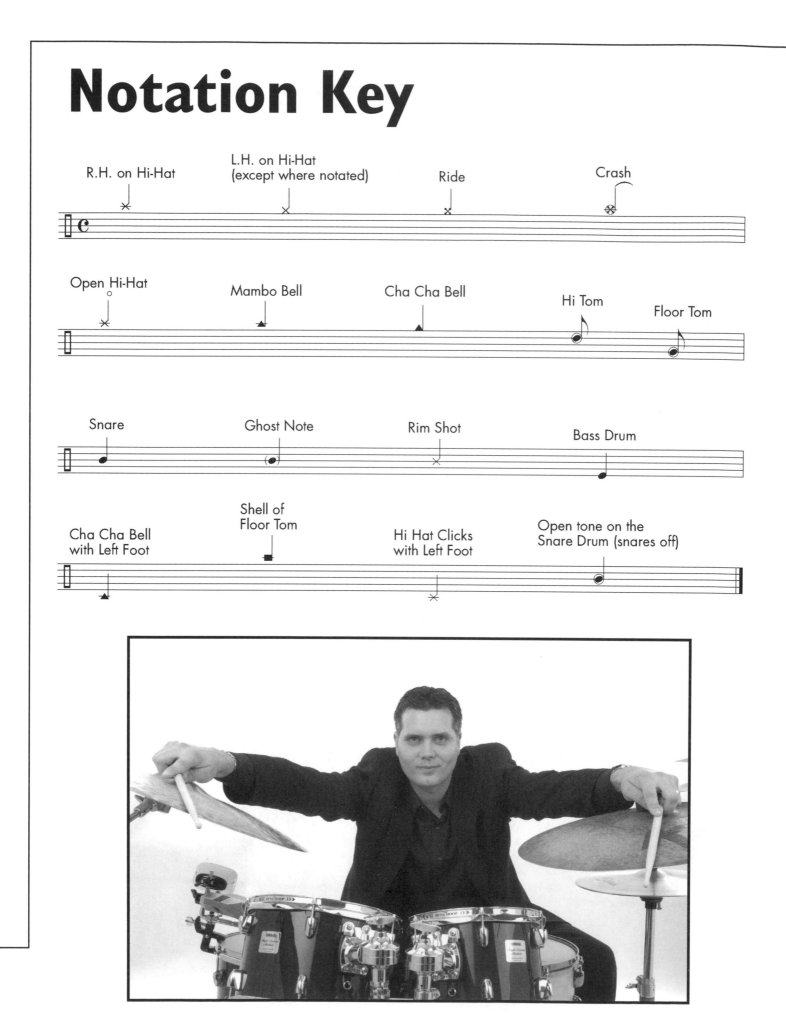

Chapter 1

The Clave

In order to understand how all of the examples presented in this book relate to Afro-Cuban drumming, we will start with the clave. The clave is a binary rhythmic pattern that serves as a foundation for the polyrhythms that are played over it. In this two-bar pattern there is one measure of three beats (known as the 3 side), and one measure of two beats (known as the 2 side). The clave can start on either side as shown in these two examples of son clave.

1. 3-2 Son Clave

2. 2-3 Son Clave

These next two variations of the clave are called rumba clave. In rumba clave there is a beat displacement of an eighth-note on the 3rd beat of the 3 side.

3. 3-2 Rumba Clave

4. 2-3 Rumba Clave

Chapter 2

The Cáscara

Now that we have an understanding of how the clave sounds, let's add the cáscara rhythm over it. *Cáscara* literally means "shell" as it refers to the shells of the timbale drums. More important, it is the syncopated rhythmic pattern played by the timbalero. When playing the cáscara pattern on the drum set, the closed hi-hat is used as a substitute for the shell sound (although the shell of the floor tom can be used as well). In Afro-Cuban music the cáscara is usually played during the verses and piano solos as it precedes the bell pattern played during the *coros* (chorus sections). These next examples demonstrate some grooves utilizing cáscara in 2-3 clave. The clave overdubs are two cycles of son clave followed by two cycles of rumba clave.

Chapter 3

The Bombo Note

Now that we've seen how the cáscara rhythm fits over the clave, the next step in this learning process is to add the bass drum. The bass drum pattern is based on the bombo note, which is the "and" of beat 2. In relation to the clave the bombo note is the second hit of the 3 side, but it can be played on the 2 side as well. The roots of the bombo are found in comparsa music, also known as conga. The following examples are cáscara patterns utilizing the bass drum to play the bombo note along with some variations.

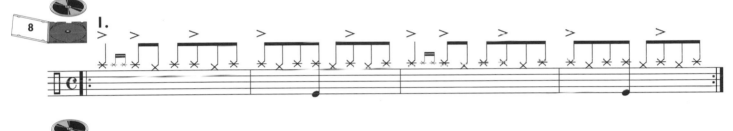

Bombo note on both sides of the clave:

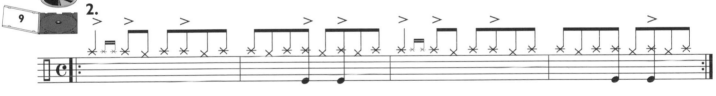

5.

6.

7.

Chapter 4

Hi-Hat Variations

As stated earlier, the cáscara pattern is usually played during verses and certain solo situations. However, using a maraca pattern adds variation to the cáscara pattern. The next four examples show the maraca pattern on a closed hi-hat using alternate sticking. As in the other examples in this book, variations of the bombo note are applied.

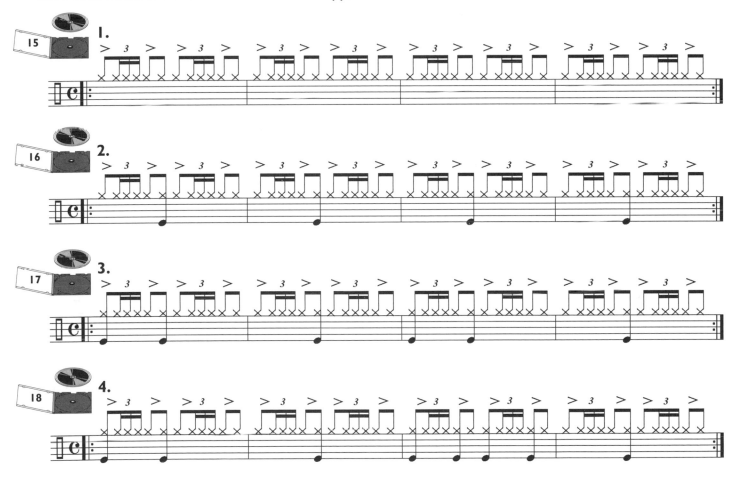

The following examples add the left hand. Within these examples, the left hand can play ghost notes, rim shots, or a combination of both as in example 6.

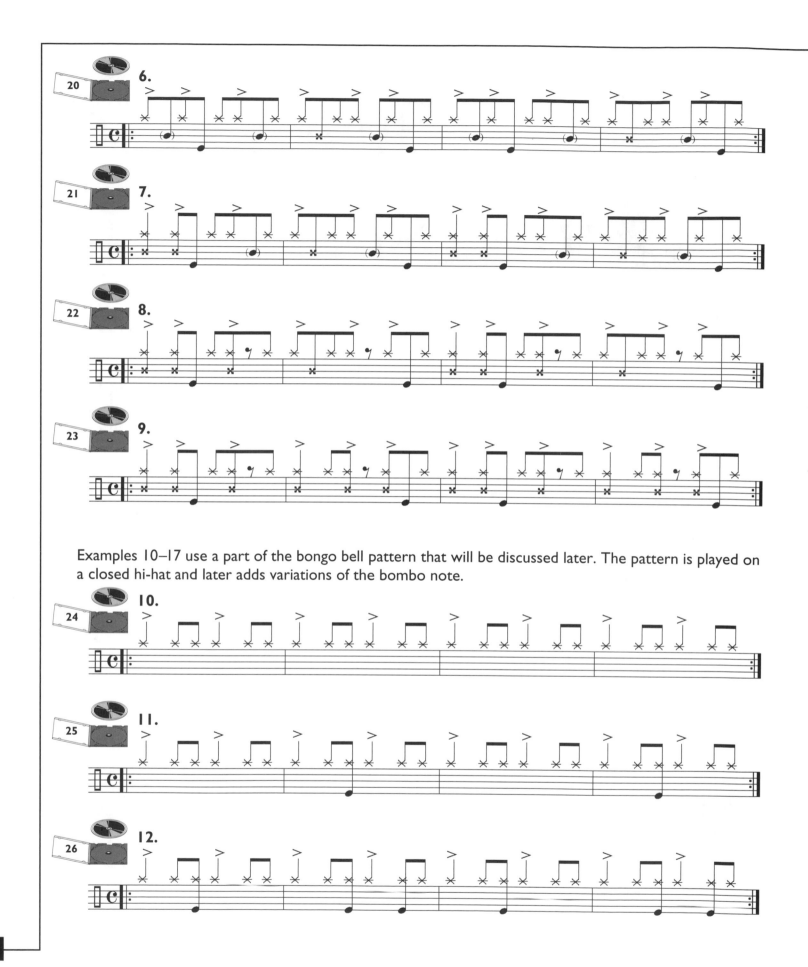

Examples 10–17 use a part of the bongo bell pattern that will be discussed later. The pattern is played on a closed hi-hat and later adds variations of the bombo note.

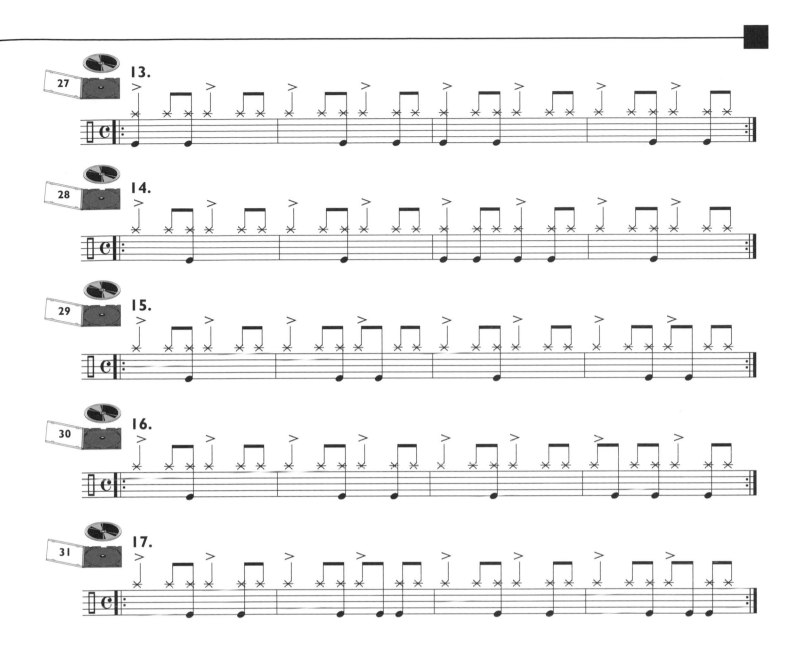

In examples 18–21 the bass drum is played on beats 3 and 4 of each measure. Doing so creates a rhythm dominant in a more recent style of Afro-Cuban music known as timba.

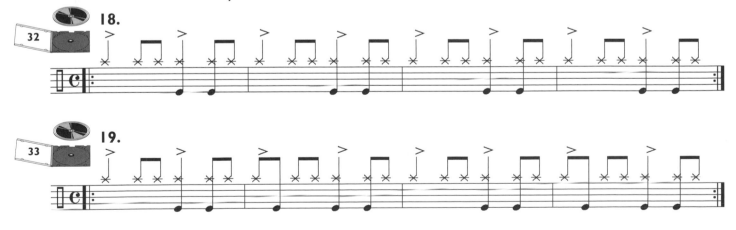

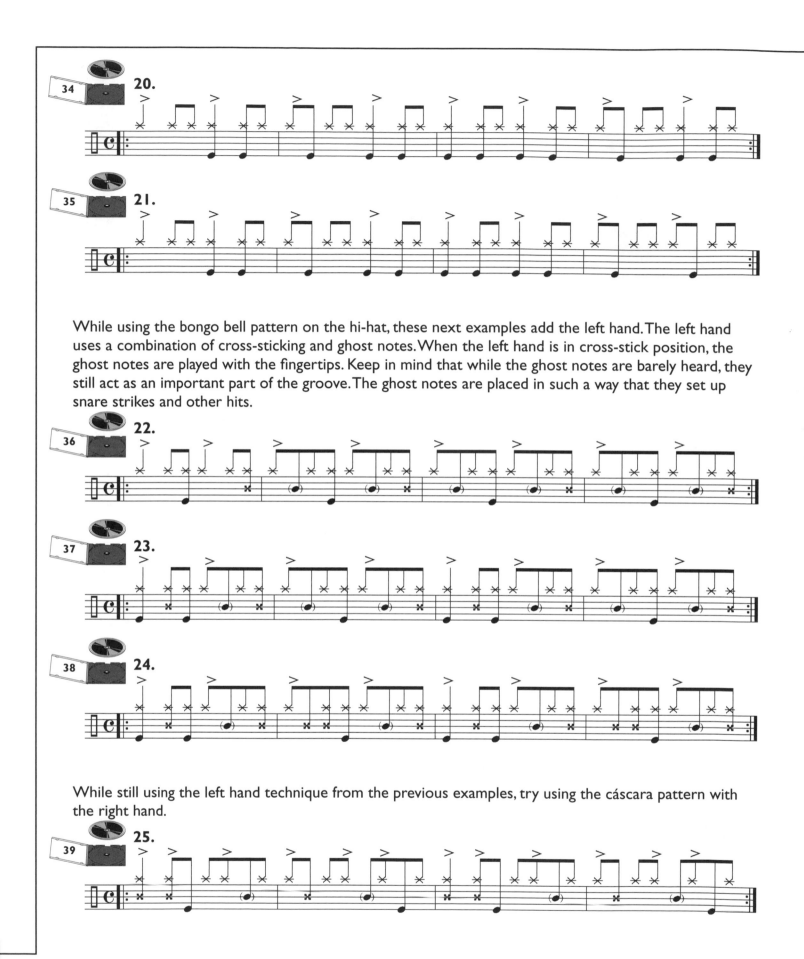

While using the bongo bell pattern on the hi-hat, these next examples add the left hand. The left hand uses a combination of cross-sticking and ghost notes. When the left hand is in cross-stick position, the ghost notes are played with the fingertips. Keep in mind that while the ghost notes are barely heard, they still act as an important part of the groove. The ghost notes are placed in such a way that they set up snare strikes and other hits.

While still using the left hand technique from the previous examples, try using the cáscara pattern with the right hand.

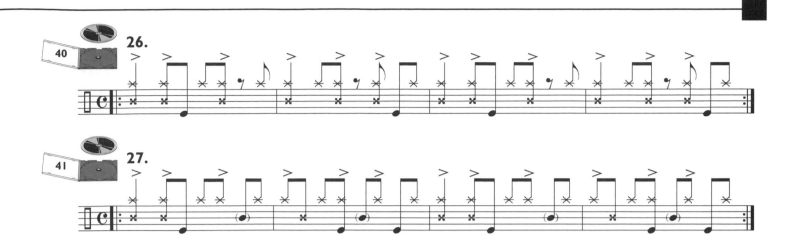

Examples 28–30 incorporate everything learned so far plus an added hi-hat opening on beat 3 of the first and third measure.

Chapter 5

The Bongo Bell

Examples 1–9 incorporate the bongo bell pattern. In Afro-Cuban music, the bongo bell usually accompanies the timbale bell during the coro sections as well as the mambo sections. Keep in mind that in this pattern, the bell is played in two spots on the bell: the open end, which is notated with an *O*, and the closed end which is also the neck of the bell, which is notated with an *N*. As in other examples, the bombo note and variations with the left hand will be added.

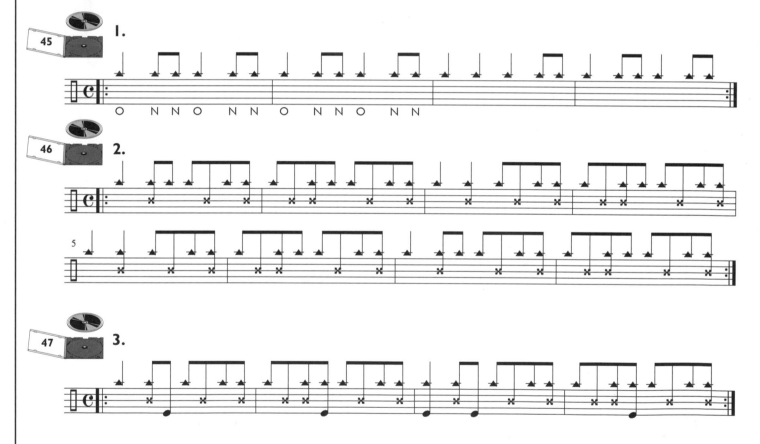

4.

5.

6.

The tom-tom notes in the second measure are played with the left hand as are all tom-tom notes, except where notated.

7.

8.

Example 9 uses the bongo bell pattern on the ride cymbal. The *B* means to strike the "bell" of the cymbal. All other cymbal strikes should be placed just underneath the bell.

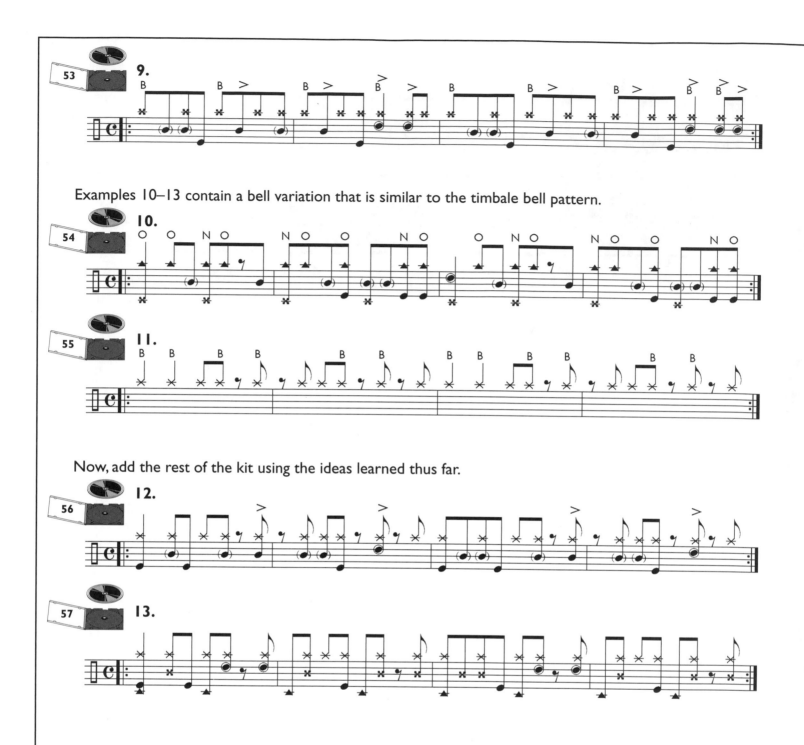

Examples 10–13 contain a bell variation that is similar to the timbale bell pattern.

Now, add the rest of the kit using the ideas learned thus far.

Bass Drum Combinations

This example incorporates numerous bass drum variations played over the bongo bell pattern. The clave overdubs are in 2-3 rumba clave.

Bass Drum Combinations (cont.)

Chapter 6

Ideas for Soloing

The following examples feature hand exercises to develop a feel for how "up beat" eighth-notes fit, in relation to clave. In these patterns, the left hand plays 3-2 rumba clave while the right hand plays around the kit. Keep in mind that the right hand can hit any drum as long as the rhythm is played as written. All examples have four-bar intros—two clave cycles.

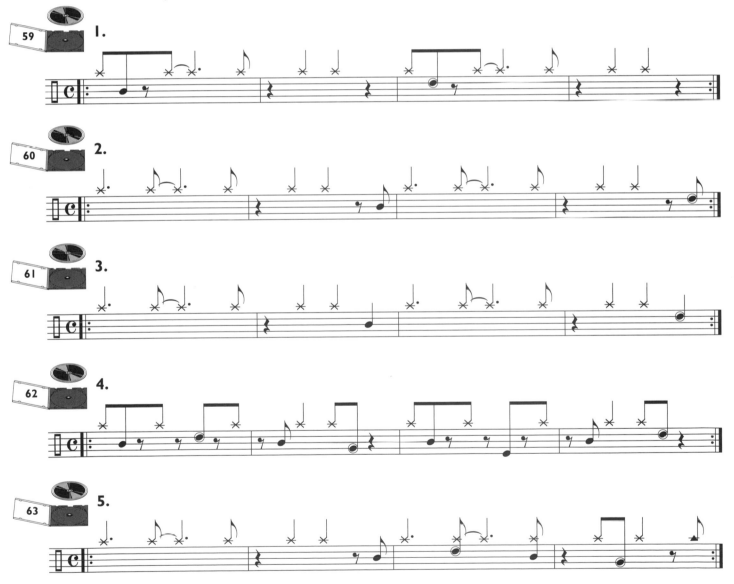

In examples 8 and 9, the left hand plays the clave while the right hand and right foot play the double-stroke triplets.

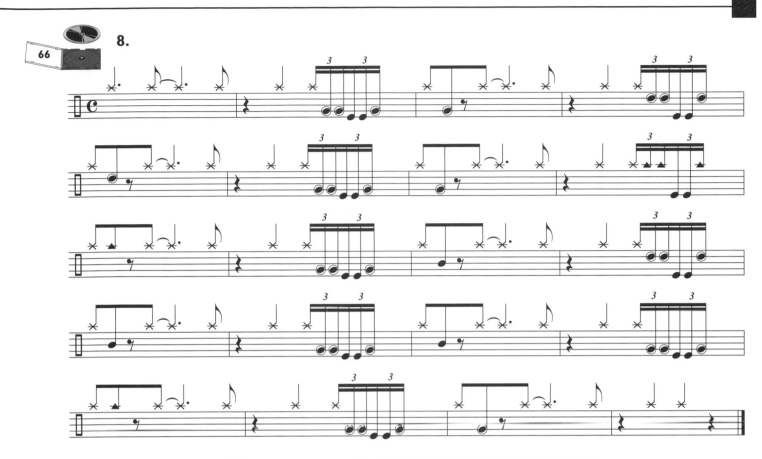

8.

9.

Chapter 7

Guaguancó

Guaguancó is one of the three main styles of rumba. The rumba cycle also consists of yambú and columbia. Any one of these three styles can be fused with contemporary Afro-Cuban music but guaguancó seems to be the most popular choice due to its 4/4 time signature and flexibility in tempo. The following examples demonstrate how to incorporate the guaguancó rhythm on the drum set. The left hand is in the cross-stick position playing the clave pattern while the right hand taps out the ghost notes. In the second measure the left hand lifts the stick up to allow the open tones to ring. (See photos.)

Notice in the first measure of example 1 that the left hand rests to muffle the sound. This technique is illustrated above.

Notice in the second measure of example 1 that the left hand comes up to allow the tone to ring. This technique is illustrated above.

68 1.

While maintaining the bass drum on beat 4, try adding beats with the hi-hat on the 1 of each measure.

In example 4, the right hand shifts to the floor tom on the "and" of beat 2, starting on the third measure.

Example 5 uses the cowbell played with the left foot. Also notice the tempo change to half note = 140.

Chapter 8

Cha Cha Cha

In the 1940s, Cuban violinist Enrique Jorrin noticed a particular sound coming from the dancers' feet when the band got to the mambo section of a danzón, a popular Cuban style from the late 19th and early 20th centuries. With this sound in mind, he created what is known today as the cha cha cha. The next five examples incorporate the cha cha cha rhythm starting with the basic pattern, and moving to a more modern Latin-funk groove. Keep in mind that each of these examples has a one-bar intro. Examples 1–3 use a pickup known as an abanico. The abanico functions as a call for the cowbells to enter. To translate it literally, *abanico* means "fan," because the drum roll sounds like a fan being opened.

1.

Traditionally, the cha cha cha bell pattern is straight quarter notes; however variations do apply. The next examples add variation to the bell as well as cross-stick rim shots, tom-tom hits, and bass drum hits on the bombo note.

2.

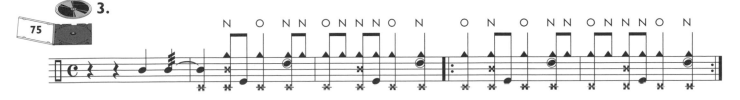

Example 3 adds the hi-hat playing four quarter notes in each measure with the left foot. Also take notice of the bell pattern variation.

3.

Other than 6/8, examples 4 and 5 are the most versatile grooves as they lend themselves to a variety of genres. With snare hits on beat 3 of every measure, and the bass drum hitting the 1, these grooves easily lend themselves to the many styles that are based on this concept, including rock, funk, and R&B.

Chapter 9

Afro-Cuban 6/8

While examples 4 and 5 on the previous page are versatile grooves, Afro-Cuban 6/8 is considered the most versatile because it can be incorporated into rock, funk, shuffle, and jazz. Based on Afro-Cuban folkloric styles, the 6/8 clave lies underneath the following grooves whether it is played or just felt.

78 **1.** Afro Cuban 6/8 Clave

79 **2.** Afro Cuban 6/8 Bell Pattern

80 **3.** Bell Variation

81 **4.** Add bass drum, snare, and hi-hat.

82 **5.**

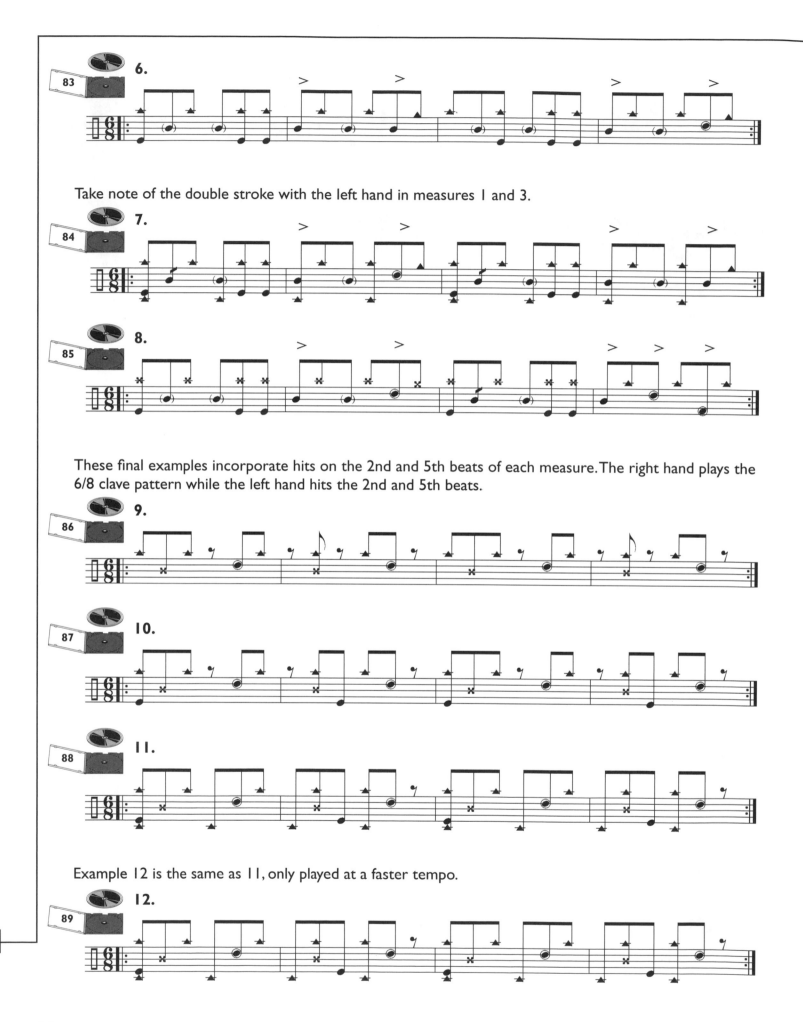

Take note of the double stroke with the left hand in measures 1 and 3.

These final examples incorporate hits on the 2nd and 5th beats of each measure. The right hand plays the 6/8 clave pattern while the left hand hits the 2nd and 5th beats.

Example 12 is the same as 11, only played at a faster tempo.

Examples 13–15 use the 6/8 bell pattern in the right hand.

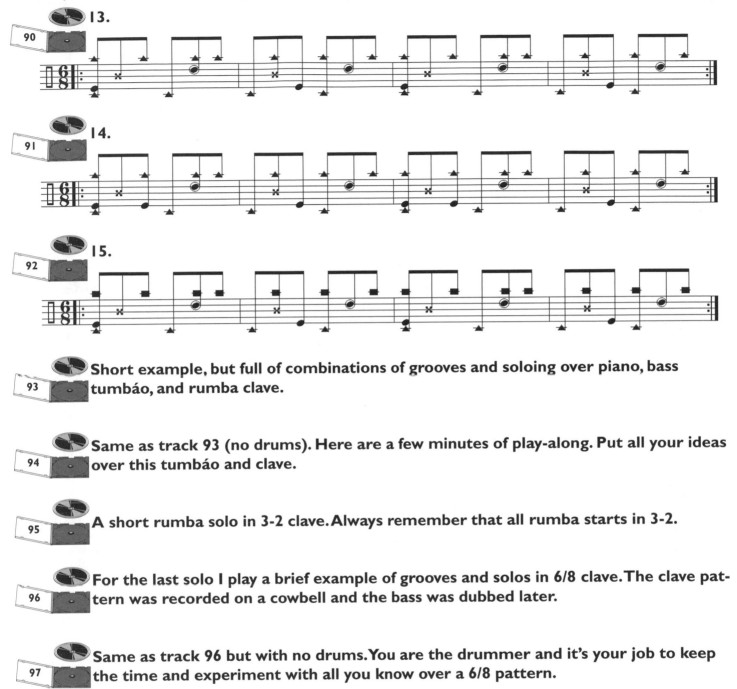

90 **13.**

91 **14.**

92 **15.**

93 Short example, but full of combinations of grooves and soloing over piano, bass tumbáo, and rumba clave.

94 Same as track 93 (no drums). Here are a few minutes of play-along. Put all your ideas over this tumbáo and clave.

95 A short rumba solo in 3-2 clave. Always remember that all rumba starts in 3-2.

96 For the last solo I play a brief example of grooves and solos in 6/8 clave. The clave pattern was recorded on a cowbell and the bass was dubbed later.

97 Same as track 96 but with no drums. You are the drummer and it's your job to keep the time and experiment with all you know over a 6/8 pattern.